Sally

Lehrwerk für den
Englischunterricht ab Klasse 3

Schülerbuch 4

Erarbeitet von
Martina Bredenbröcker
Daniela Elsner
Stefanie Gleixner-Weyrauch
Simone Gutwerk
Marion Lugauer

Unter Beratung von Jane Brockmann-Fairchild

Illustriert von
Monica May, Wilfried Poll,
Anja Boretzki, Andreas Fischer,
Thilo Pustlauk und Gisela Vogel

Oldenbourg

Inhalt

Special days:

 pupil's CD / teacher's CD

teacher's CD only

Write.

Draw.

Speak.

Rap: Welcome back to school!

Step to the left, step to the right.

Raise your  and feel alright.

Turn around and say: "That's cool!"

Welcome back to school!

Sit on your , write in the air.

Let's have fun with English.

Dance to the beat and say: "That's cool!"

Welcome back to school!

Around the classroom you must look.

Put your  on the .

Turn around and say: "That's cool!"

Welcome back to school!

 Listen and sing.

Let's play a board game!

Play in groups of 5.
Roll the dice. Take turns.

Red number:
Do what it says or answer the question.
If you can't, miss a turn.

The winner is the first to reach
number 80.

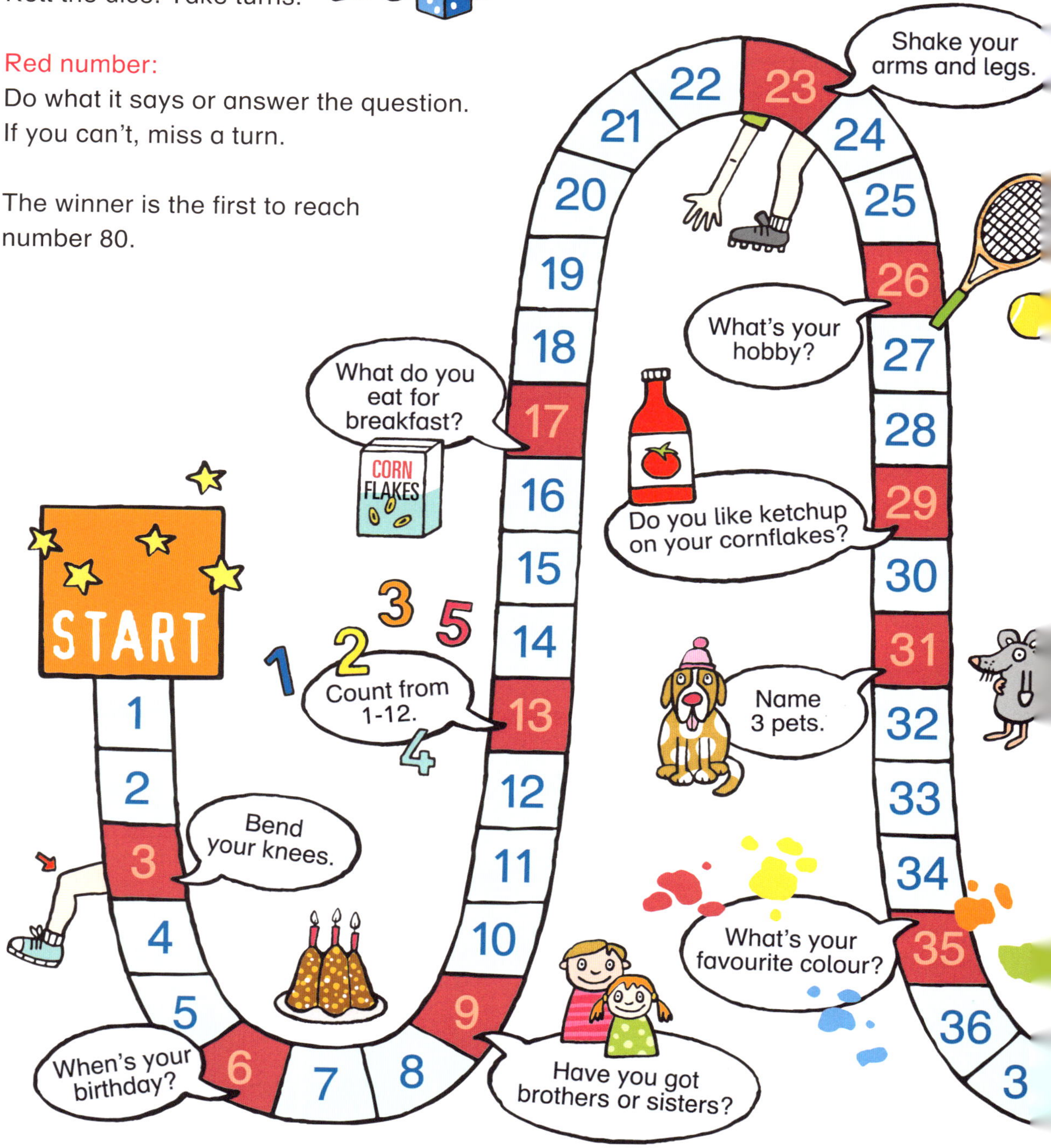

Shake your arms and legs.

22 23 24 25

21 20 19 18

26 27 28 29 30

What's your hobby?

What do you eat for breakfast?

CORN FLAKES

17 16 15 14 13

Do you like ketchup on your cornflakes?

31 32 33 34 35 36 3

Name 3 pets.

3 5
2
1
Count from 1-12.
4

START

1 2 3 4 5

Bend your knees.

12 11 10 9 8 7 6

What's your favourite colour?

When's your birthday?

Have you got brothers or sisters?

Name the days of the week.

Stand on one leg for 30 seconds.

Say a rhyme or sing a song.

Name 5 things in your classroom.

Name 5 types of fruit.

What's the weather like today?

What's the name of your best friend?

Show me your socks. What colour are they?

What's your favourite toy?

What's your telephone number?

Sing a birthday song.

How do you feel today?

Who is it?

FINISH

Our home is too small

bedroom   bedroom   bathroom

garden

kitchen   living room   toilet

The ... is too small!

1. Listen to the story and point.

2. Look at the house and speak.
   The living room is too small ...

3. Draw your dream house.
   Write about it.

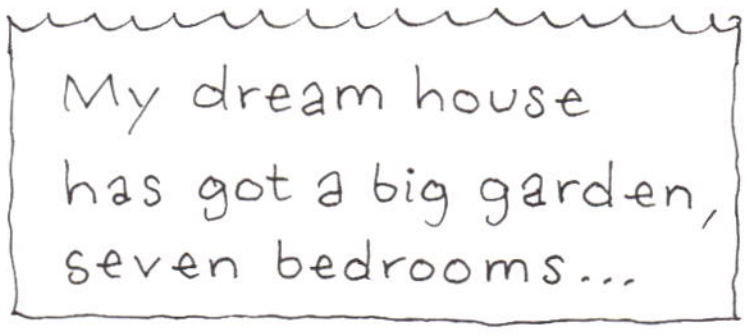

My dream house
has got a big garden,
seven bedrooms...

At home

Tim and Susan's new house

bed, chair, table,
desk, sofa,
cupboard, shelves,
stereo, lamp

door

window

 1. Listen, find Susan's furniture and point.

 2. What furniture has Susan got?
Susan has got brown shelves, a purple sofa ...

 3. What furniture have you got in your room?
I've got ...

Let's make Sally's sandwich!

You need:
bread
ketchup
mustard
a tomato
a cucumber
ham
cheese
lettuce

Take a slice of toasted bread. Put it on a plate.

Spread ketchup and mustard on it.

Cut the tomato and the cucumber.
Put them on the bread.

Put some ham, cheese and lettuce on it.

Put another slice of toasted bread on top.

Sally's sandwich is ready to eat!

Enjoy your meal!

 What do you want to put on your sandwich? Make a list.

Let's have lunch

In the dining hall

It's Monday.

It's Tuesday.

It's Thursday.

It's Friday.

 1. Listen and read.

 2. Write about Phil's menu plan.
On Monday Phil has salad with cheese and a glass of water.
On Tuesday he has …

Emily's day

At 8 o'clock I get up and have breakfast.

School begins at 9 o'clock.

At 12 o'clock I have lunch.

At 3 o'clock I go home.

At 4 o'clock I do my homework.

At 5 o'clock I call my friends and we play football.

At 6 o'clock I have dinner.

At 8 o'clock I read a book or watch TV.

At 9 o'clock I go to bed. Good night!

1. Listen, look and read.

2. What about your day? Tell your partner what you do.
   In the morning …
   In the afternoon …
   In the evening / At night …

3. And what do you do on a Sunday?

MY SUNDAY
On Sunday I get up…

Hobbies

riding a horse   riding a mountain bike   playing the guitar
reading books   ice skating   playing the piano   snowboarding
playing football   swimming

1. What are their hobbies? Look and speak.
   Tim's hobby is …

2. What's your hobby?
   My hobby is …

3. Hobbies in your class:
   Make a list and do
   a class survey.

playing football 🗋 ∄∣
reading books 📖 ∄∣

Teddy bear, teddy bear, turn around!

rope skipping

The interview

 1. Listen to the interview
   with Dirk Nowitzki.

2. Ask your partner.

Dirk Nowitzki playing basketball

Can you	play football
	sing a song
	play the guitar
	ride a skateboard
	do inline skating

?

3. Make your own interview.

4. Say the tongue twister.

I can canoe a new canoe.
Can you canoe a new canoe, too?

 **Shopping**

In the supermarket

 1. Listen and point.

2. Make your own shopping list.
   I want to buy two bottles of orange juice,
   a box of biscuits …

I like shopping!

At the shopping centre

SWEET SHOP

CHOC

ice cream

CINEMA

KING KONG

HARRY POTTER

JAMES BOND

SPORTS SHOP

T-SHIRTS £5

CAPS

JEANS & SKIRTS

COMPUTER SHOP

Where can you buy these things?

In the	book shop	I can buy
	sports shop	
	music shop	
	supermarket	
	toy shop	
	sweet shop	
	shoe shop	

Jack and the beanstalk

 1. Listen, look and point.

2. Act out the story together.

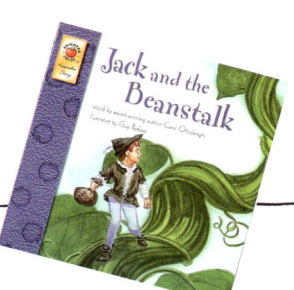

Jack and the beanstalk

Let's act it out!

Reading and learning the story

Painting the background

Making the music

Telling the story with shadow puppets

Practising the story

Performing the story

Detective Brighthead

1. Listen to the story and look at the pictures.

2. What forms of transport does Mr Brighthead take? He takes the …

 **Vehicles**

Transport in London

left-hand traffic with
double-decker buses

a taxi

an entrance to the underground trains

a ship on the River Thames

 1. Look at the photos. What's different in England?

In the plane

 No smoking!

 Switch off your mobile phones, radios and laptops!

 Fasten your seat belts, please!

 Put your seats in an upright position!

 2. Listen and point.

 3. Draw your own sign.
Ask your partner: (What is it?)

The Wright Brothers

The Wright Brothers made bikes.

The Wright Brothers made kites.

The Wright Brothers made planes.

The Wright Brothers became famous with the "Wright Model B".

1. Look and read.

a flying sledge

a bike saucer

a one-wheeled car

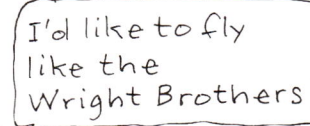

I'd like to fly like the Wright Brothers!

**2. Look at Gyro Gearloose's fantasy vehicles.
Draw your own fantasy vehicle.**

Detective Brighthead's trip to the jungle

zebra   lion   giraffe   hippo

monkey   elephant   snake   tortoise

1. Where are the animals?
   Ask your partner.

   Is the zebra next to the snake?
   Is the hippo behind the elephant? …

   | in   on   next to   in front of |
   | behind   under |

   Yes, it is.   No, it isn't. It's …

2. Make a poster.

The five minute zoo game

Play with a partner.

Roll the dice.

Play for five minutes.

Take turns.

The winner is the player who has got the most points.

Move in any direction.

Animal picture:
Name the animal = 1 point.
Name the animal and describe it = 2 points.

Snack stop: You must pay.
Miss a turn.

Crocodile: Bad luck!
You lose 1 point.

The clever tortoise

Listen, look and read.

At the doctor's

1. Read.

2. Why do the animals run away each time? Look at the green door.

The inline skating accident

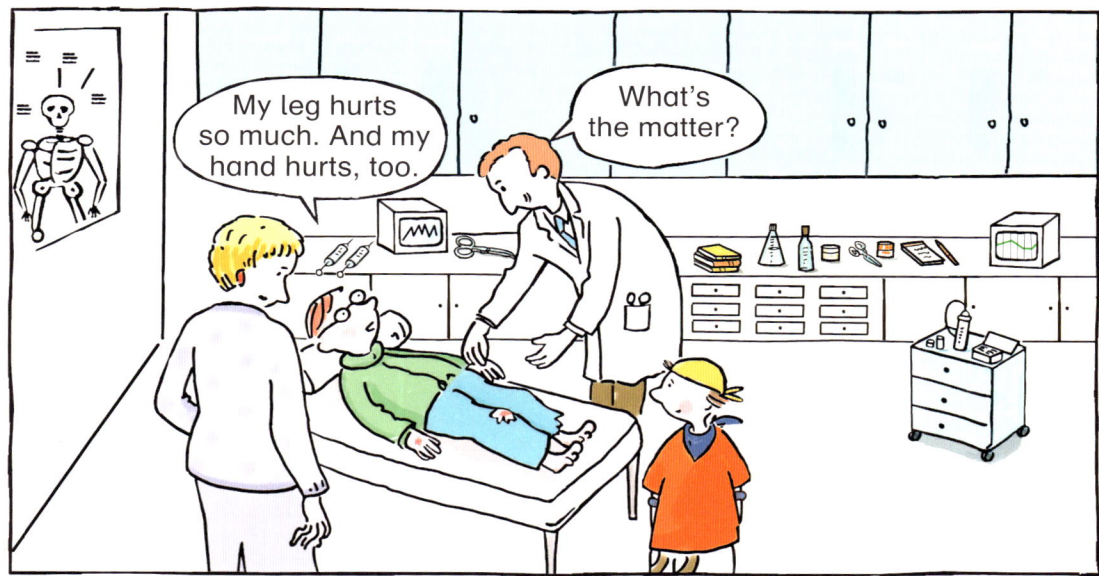

 1. Look and speak.

 2. Look at the waiting room.
   What's the matter?
   Write a sentence about each patient.
   The boy has got a headache …

headache
neckache
earache
backache

Going to Scotland

Sally and the Loch Ness Monster

Listen, look and read.

A holiday trip to Scotland

I want to see the Highland Mountains and go fishing.

I want to go to a castle.

I want to visit the Highland Games.

I want to go to the sea.

And we all want to see Nessie!

 1. Look and speak. Mr Brown wants to see …

2. Make a poster or a collage about Scotland.
   Find out and learn about Scotland in the internet.

3. Where do you want to go for your holidays?

SCOTLAND

SCOTTISH HILLS

LOCH NESS

Going to Scotland

Scottish dance

F

Left foot, right foot, up and down and then

C⁷

take your part – ner and be – gin a – gain.

F

Right foot, left foot, up and down and then

C⁷   F

clap your hands and stop!

Today I'm wearing my skirt!

Listen, sing and dance.

What do you want to be?

shop assistant

hairdresser

policewoman

doctor

teacher

millionaire

 1. What do you want to be?
I want to be a …

 2. Do a job survey in your class.
Make a chart from it.

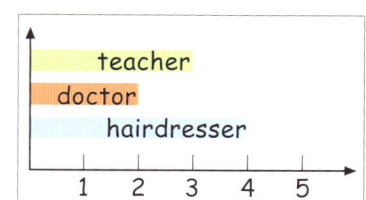

My jobs

I have to help in the garden.

I have to make my bed.

I have to do my homework.

I have to feed the cat.

I have to walk the dog.

I have to tidy my room.

I have to help in the kitchen.

And what are your jobs?
I have to …

My cat likes to hide in boxes

France

Japan

Spain

Berlin, Germany

Greece

 1. Listen and look.

 2. Mime one of the cats.
Let your partner guess.

 Are you from …?

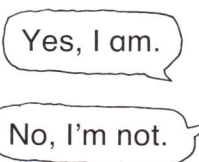 Yes, I am.

No, I'm not.

Meeting people

We all live in the same world

Hola! — Juanita

Bonjour! — Jacqueline

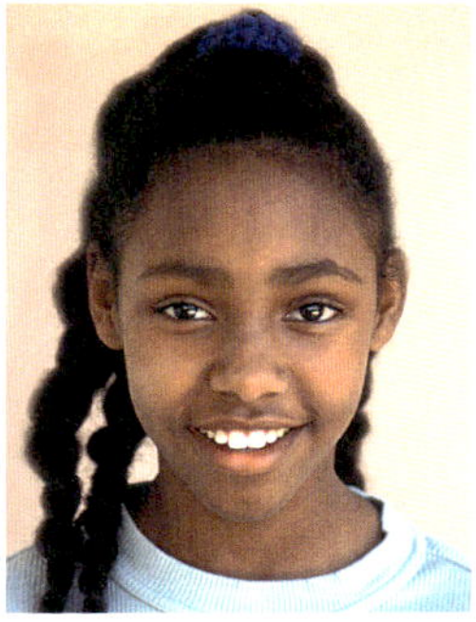

Ciao! — Paolo

Hello! — Thomas

Hallo! — Maria

Merhaba! — Güler

Jassu! — Dimitra

Priwjet! — Sergej

But we all laugh in the same language.
We all like to sing and play.
We all live in the same world,
no matter where we're from.

 1. Listen and sing.

2. What's the word for (Hello!)
   in different languages?
   Make a list.

Are you from Japan, too?

No, I'm not. I'm from Australia!

Looking for a penfriend

Datei Bearbeiten Ansicht Favoriten Extras ?

Zurück ▾ ⏹ Suchen ⭐ Favoriten   Adresse ▾ Wechseln zu Links

Find a penfriend!

I'm a | boy | .   I'm | 8 | years old.   I'm from | Germany | .
| girl | | 9 | | England |
                      | 10 | | Australia |

My hobby is | snowboarding | .

I'm looking for a | boy | .   Age: | 8 | Country: | USA |
                  | girl | | 9 | | Germany |
                                     | 10 | | Spain |

Carlos: boy, 10 years old, Spain

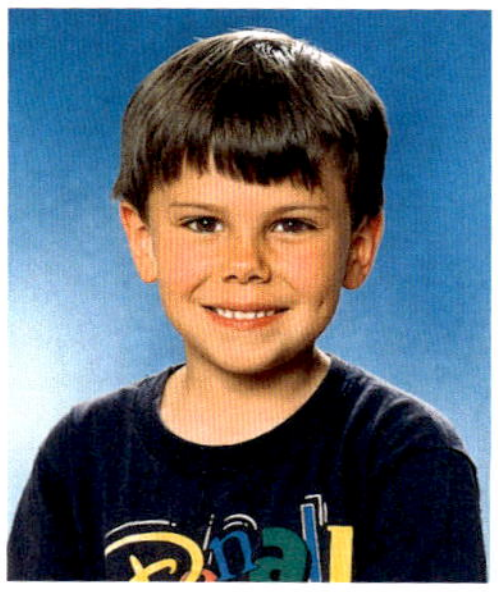

Hi, I'm Carlos. I'm from Spain.
I'm 10 years old.
My hobbies are skateboarding,
reading comics and swimming.
I can speak Spanish, German and English.
I'm looking for a penfriend from England.

 1. Listen. What is Phil looking for? Tell your class.
   He's looking for a ... from ...

2. Are you looking for a penfriend, too? (Yes, I'm looking for a ...) (No, I don't want a penfriend.)
   Tell your partner.

3. Write a letter to Carlos.

Dear Carlos,
I'm ...

(Where is the mouse? I want to catch it.)

Guy Fawkes

Guy Fawkes Day – Bonfire Night

Light the fire, light the fire.
Let it burn, let it burn.
Bonfire, bonfire.
Guy Fawkes Day, Guy Fawkes Day.

Sizzle, whistle, sizzle, whistle.
Crackle, rumble, crackle, rumble.
Boom, bang, boom, bang.
Fireworks, fireworks.

 1. Listen and sing.

 2. Write the seasons in the correct order.
autumn ...

winter   summer

autumn   spring

Thanksgiving today

Mum gets up at 6 o'clock
in the morning.
She puts the turkey into the oven.
The turkey takes five hours to cook.

At 12 o'clock my grandpa,
my grandma, my aunt and
my cousins come to our house.
We have our Thanksgiving dinner.

In the afternoon we go to the
Thanksgiving parade.

In the evening we watch the football
match on TV.

My name is Carol.
This is my
Thanksgiving Day.
What do you celebrate
in your country?

A turkey is a funny bird,
his head goes wobble, wobble.
And he knows just one word:
"Gobble, gobble, gobble!"

 Listen, look and read.

A story about the first Thanksgiving

1. What do you know about the American Indians?
2. What is Sally writing?

Come to the USA!

New York and the Statue of Liberty

Disney World, Florida (fun park)

a cowboy at a rodeo

Bryce Canyon National Park, Utah

a cable car in San Francisco

Venice Beach, Los Angeles

I'm going to show you the USA!

1. Look at the photos.

2. Make a poster or a collage about the USA.
   Find out and learn about the USA in the internet.

Christmas in Australia

Father Christmas in Australia

 1. Listen and point.

2. Read.

The five days of Christmas

On the first day of Christmas
my true love sent to me
a in a gum tree.

On the second day of Christmas
my true love sent to me

two small

and a  in a gum tree.

koala

kookaburra

On the third day of Christmas
my true love sent to me

three  ,

two small …

cockatoo

On the fourth day of Christmas
my true love sent to me

four  ,

three …

crocodile

On the fifth day of Christmas
my true love sent to me

five  ,

four …

kangaroo

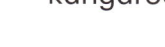 1. Look at the photos. Listen and sing.

2. Write word cards for a Christmas bingo.
   sleigh, reindeer, stocking, present, star,
   Christmas tree, winter, cold, snowy...

Let's go to Australia!

Sydney

a road train

Ayers Rock

the Great Barrier Reef

an Australian Aborigine playing the didgeridoo

1. Look at the photos.

 2. Listen and point.

3. Read the text.

4. Draw an Australian traffic sign.

Easter

Let's make an Easter bunny mosaic card!

You need:
coloured egg shells
cardboard
a pencil
glue

Break the egg shells
into small pieces.

Draw your Easter bunny
on the cardboard.

Glue the egg shells down
to make your mosaic bunny.

Glue your Easter bunny onto the
cardboard. Write an Easter greeting
on your card.

✏ Write word cards for an Easter bingo.
bunny, egg, tree, flower, grass,
spring, warm, cloudy, sunny ...

Words

Africa Afrika
afternoon der Nachmittag
America Amerika
I am ich bin
angry wütend
animal das Tier
animal centre das Tierheim
apple der Apfel
April der April
they are sie sind
we are wir sind
you are du bist, ihr seid
arm der Arm
arrow der Pfeil
Asia Asien
August der August
aunt die Tante
Australia Australien
autumn der Herbst
away weg

backache die Rückenschmerzen
bacon der Speck
bad schlecht, schlimm
ball der Ball
banana die Banane
basket der Korb
bat die Fledermaus
bathroom das Badezimmer
to be sein
beach der Strand
beachball der Wasserball
bean die Bohne
beanstalk die Bohnenranke

bear der Bär
bed das Bett
bedroom das Schlafzimmer
behind hinter
to bend beugen
big groß
bird der Vogel
birthday der Geburtstag
biscuit der Keks
black schwarz
blood das Blut
blue blau
board die Tafel
body der Körper
book das Buch
boot der Stiefel
bottle die Flasche
bow der Bogen
box (boxes) die Schachtel
(die Schachteln), die Kiste (die Kisten)
boy der Junge, der Bub
bread das Brot
breakfast das Frühstück
brother der Bruder
brown braun
to brush bürsten
budgie der Wellensittich
bus (buses) der Bus (die Busse)
butter die Butter
to buy kaufen

cake der Kuchen
to call rufen, anrufen
can können
can't nicht können
Canada Kanada
candle die Kerze
cap die Kappe

Words

car   das Auto
card   die Karte
carrot   die Karotte, die Möhre
castle   das Schloss, die Burg
cat   die Katze
to catch   fangen
chair   der Stuhl
chalk   die Kreide
cheap   billig
cheese   der Käse
cherry (cherries)
die Kirsche (die Kirschen)
child   das Kind
children   die Kinder
chimney   der Schornstein
chocolate bar   der Schokoriegel
Christmas   Weihnachten
Christmas tree
der Weihnachtsbaum, der Christbaum
to clap   klatschen
class   die Klasse
to clean   putzen
clever   schlau, klug
to climb   klettern, hochklettern
(one) o'clock   (ein) Uhr
clothes   die Kleidung
cloud   die Wolke
cloudy   bewölkt
coat   der Mantel
coffee   der Kaffee
coke   die Cola
cold   kalt
colour   die Farbe
to colour   anmalen
to come   kommen
computer   der Computer
computer game   das Computerspiel
cookie   der Keks
corn   der Mais
cornflakes   die Cornflakes
costume   die Verkleidung

to count   zählen
cousin   der Cousin, die Cousine
cow   die Kuh
cucumber   die Gurke
a cup of ...   eine Tasse ...
cupboard   der Schrank
to cut   schneiden

to dance   tanzen
dark   dunkel
day   der Tag
December   der Dezember
desk   der Schreibtisch
dice   der Würfel
dirty   schmutzig
to do   machen, tun
to do magic   zaubern
doctor   der Arzt
dog   der Hund
doll   die Puppe
door   die Tür
down   hinunter
to draw   zeichnen
dress   das Kleid
drink   das Getränk
to drink   trinken
duck   die Ente

ear   das Ohr
earache   die Ohrenschmerzen
Easter   Ostern
Easter bunny   der Osterhase
Easter egg   das Osterei
to eat   essen
egg   das Ei
eight   acht

Words

elephant der Elefant
eleven elf
England England
English englisch
Englishman der Engländer
Europe Europa
evening der Abend
exercise die Übung
expensive teuer
eye das Auge

fairy die Fee
family die Familie
farm animal das Bauernhoftier
fast schnell
fat dick, fett
father der Vater
Father Christmas
der Weihnachtsmann
favourite (pet) Lieblings(tier)
February der Februar
to feed füttern
feet die Füße
ferry die Fähre
to fill füllen
fine gut, schön
finger der Finger
fireplace der Kamin
fish der Fisch, die Fische
five fünf
floor der Fußboden
flower die Blume
fly die Fliege
to fly fliegen
fog der Nebel
foggy nebelig
folder der Schnellhefter
food das Essen

foot der Fuß
football der Fußball
forest der Wald
fork die Gabel
four vier
France Frankreich
Friday der Freitag
friend der Freund, die Freundin
friendly freundlich
frog der Frosch
fruit die Frucht, das Obst
fruit salad der Obstsalat
fun der Spaß
funny lustig, komisch

game das Spiel
garage die Garage
garden der Garten
German deutsch
Germany Deutschland
to get up aufstehen
ghost der Geist
giraffe die Giraffe
girl das Mädchen
a glass of ... ein Glas ...
glue der Kleber
to go gehen, fahren
good gut
goose die Gans
grandfather der Großvater
grandmother die Großmutter
grass das Gras
Great Britain Großbritannien
green grün
grey grau
guard die Wache
guinea pig das Meerschweinchen
guitar die Gitarre**

Words

hair   das Haar
Halloween   Halloween
ham   der Schinken
hamster   der Hamster
hand   die Hand
happy   glücklich
hat   der Hut
to have (got)   haben
to have (lunch)   (zu Mittag) essen
head   der Kopf
headache   die Kopfschmerzen
to help   helfen
hen   die Henne
hill   der Hügel
hippo   das Nilpferd
holidays   die Ferien
hobby (hobbies)   das Hobby (die Hobbys)
home   das Heim, das Zuhause
at home   zu Hause
homework   die Hausaufgaben
honey   der Honig
horse   das Pferd
hot chocolate   der Kakao
hot   heiß
house   das Haus
hungry   hungrig
to hurt   wehtun

ice cream   das Eis
ice skating   das Schlittschuhfahren
in front of   vor
in   in
inline skates   die Inlineskates
insect   das Insekt

jacket   die Jacke
jam   die Marmelade
January   der Januar
Japan   Japan
jeans   die Jeans
job   die Arbeit, die Aufgabe
July   der Juli
to jump   springen
June   der Juni

kangaroo   das Känguru
ketchup   das Ketchup
king   der König
kitchen   die Küche
knee   das Knie
knife (knives)   das Messer (die Messer)
to knock   klopfen
to know   wissen, kennen

Words

ladder   die Leiter
lake   der See
lamp   die Lampe
leaf (leaves)   das Blatt (die Blätter)
to learn   lernen
left   links
leg   das Bein
lemon   die Zitrone
lemonade   die Limonade
letter   der Brief
lettuce   der Kopfsalat
to like   mögen
lion   der Löwe
to listen (to)   zuhören
little   klein
to live   leben, wohnen
living room   das Wohnzimmer
to love   lieben, sehr mögen
lunch   das Mittagessen

magic (beans)   Zauber(bohnen)
to make   machen
March   der März
market   der Markt
May   der Mai
meadow   die Wiese
to meet   treffen, begegnen
melon   die Melone
mice   die Mäuse
milk   die Milch
mitten   der Fäustling
Monday   der Montag
money   das Geld
monkey   der Affe
month   der Monat

monster   das Ungeheuer
moon   der Mond
morning   der Morgen
mother   die Mutter
mountain   der Berg
mountain bike   das Mountainbike
mouse   die Maus
mouth   der Mund
to move   (sich) bewegen
must   müssen
mustard   der Senf

name   der Name
neckache   die Nackenschmerzen
new   neu
New Zealand   Neuseeland
next to   neben
night   die Nacht
nine   neun
nose   die Nase
November   der November
number   die Zahl

October   der Oktober
old   alt
on   auf
one   eins
orange   die Orange; orange
orange juice   der Orangensaft

Words

to paint malen
palace der Palast
parents die Eltern
park der Park
to pay bezahlen
pear die Birne
pen der Füller
pencil der Bleistift
pencil case das Mäppchen
people die Leute, die Merschen
pepper der Pfeffer
pet das Haustier
piano das Klavier
picture das Bild
pie die Pastete, der Kuchen
pig das Schwein
pineapple die Ananas
pink rosa
plane das Flugzeug
plate der Teller
to play spielen
player der Spieler
please bitte
plum die Pflaume
pond der Teich
poor arm
potato (potatoes)
die Kartoffel (die Kartoffeln)
present das Geschenk
prince der Prinz
princess die Prinzessin
pullover der Pullover
pumpkin der Kürbis
pupil der Schüler
purple lila
to put setzen, stellen, legen
to put on anziehen

queen die Königin

rabbit das Kaninchen
rain der Regen
rainy regnerisch
to read lesen
red rot
reindeer das Rentier, die Rentiere
rich reich
to ride fahren, reiten
right rechts
river der Fluss
roll das Brötchen, die Semmel
room das Zimmer
rubber der Radiergummi
ruler das Lineal
to run rennen, laufen

sad traurig
salt das Salz
sand der Sand
sandwich das Sandwich
Saturday der Samstag
scared erschrocken, ängstlich
scarf der Schal
school die Schule
schoolbag die Schultasche
scissors die Schere
Scotland Schottland
sea das Meer, die See
seashell die Muschel

Words

season   die Jahreszeit
to see   sehen
to sell   verkaufen
September   der September
seven   sieben
to shake   schütteln
sheep   das Schaf
shelves   das Regal
sheriff   der Sheriff
to shine   scheinen
ship   das Schiff
shoe   der Schuh
shop   das Geschäft, der Laden
shopping   der Einkauf, das Einkaufen
short   kurz
shorts   die kurze Hose
shoulder   die Schulter
to show   zeigen
sick   krank
to sing   singen
sister   die Schwester
six   sechs
skirt   der Rock
sleigh   der (Pferde-)Schlitten
slow   langsam
small   klein
to smell   riechen
snake   die Schlange
to snorkel   schnorcheln, tauchen
snow   der Schnee
snowboarding   das Snowboarden
snowman   der Schneemann
snowy   verschneit
sock   die Socke
sofa   das Sofa
song   das Lied
I'm sorry!   Entschuldigung!
soup   die Suppe
spaceship   das Raumschiff
Spain   Spanien
to speak   sprechen

spider   die Spinne
spinach   der Spinat
spoon   der Löffel
sports   Sport
spring   der Frühling
stairs   die Treppe
to stamp   stampfen
star   der Stern
stereo   die Musikanlage
stocking   der Strumpf
story   die Geschichte
strong   stark
sugar   der Zucker
summer   der Sommer
sun   die Sonne
Sunday   der Sonntag
sunglasses   die Sonnenbrille
sunny   sonnig
sweatshirt   das Sweatshirt
sweet   süß
sweets   die Süßigkeiten
to swim   schwimmen

table   der Tisch
tadpole   die Kaulquappe
to take   nehmen
to take off   ausziehen
tall   groß
taxi   das Taxi
tea   der Tee
teacher   der Lehrer, die Lehrerin
teddy bear   der Teddybär
teeth   die Zähne
ten   zehn
Thank you!   Danke!
Thanksgiving Day   das Erntedankfest
thirsty   durstig
three   drei

Words

Thursday   der Donnerstag
to tidy   aufräumen, saubermachen
tired   müde
toast   der Toast
toe   der Zeh
toilet   die Toilette, das Klo
tomato (tomatoes)
die Tomate (die Tomaten)
tooth   der Zahn
tortoise   die Schildkröte
to touch   anfassen
towel   das Handtuch
toy   das Spielzeug
train   der Zug
tree   der Baum
trousers   die Hose
T-shirt   das T-Shirt
Tuesday   der Dienstag
turkey   der Truthahn
twelve   zwölf
two   zwei

uncle   der Onkel
under   unter
underground   die U-Bahn
unhappy   unglücklich
Union Jack   britische Fahne
United States of America
die Vereinigten Staaten von Amerika, die
USA
up   hinauf

Valentine's Day   der Valentinstag
vehicle   das Fahrzeug, das Verkehrsmittel

to walk   gehen, wandern
to walk the dog
den Hund spazieren führen
to write   schreiben
warm   warm
water   das Wasser
to wash   waschen
wax figure   die Wachsfigur
to wear   tragen
weather   das Wetter
weather forecast
die Wettervorhersage
Wednesday   der Mittwoch
white   weiß
wild   wild
wind   der Wind
window   das Fenster
windy   windig
winter   der Winter
witch   die Hexe
woolly hat   die Mütze
word   das Wort
workbook   das Arbeitsheft

yellow   gelb

**Der produktive Wortschatz
(Minimalwortschatz) ist rot gedruckt.**